# THE HIGHER CRITICISM

Wipf and Stock Publishers
199 W 8th Ave, Suite 3
Eugene, OR 97401

The Higher Criticism
Four Papers
By Driver, Samuel R. and Kirkpatrick, A. F.
Softcover ISBN-13: 978-1-6667-6172-6
Hardcover ISBN-13: 978-1-6667-6173-3
eBook ISBN-13: 978-1-6667-6174-0
Publication date 10/10/2022
Previously published by Hodder and Stoughton, 1912

# THE HIGHER CRITICISM

## ꬰour ꬰapers

BY

## S. R. DRIVER, D.D.

*Canon of Christ Church, and Regius Professor of Hebrew, Oxford.*

AND

## A. F. KIRKPATRICK, D.D.

*DEAN OF ELY*

*(sometime Master of Selwyn College and Lady Margaret's Professor of Divinity, Cambridge).*

WIPF & STOCK · Eugene, Oregon

# PREFACE

THE first, third and fourth of the following papers were originally reprinted six years ago, in 1905, in the hope that they might help to remove some of the misconceptions which, as various articles and letters in the public papers had shewn at the time, prevailed widely with regard to the nature and scope of the "Higher Criticism." I had already decided to reprint my own two papers with this view, when it occurred to me that the paper read by my colleague, Professor Kirkpatrick, of Cambridge, now Dean of Ely, at the Northampton Church Congress in 1902, would form a valuable addition to them; and I am grateful to him for the ready assent which he gave to my proposal that this paper should be included with mine. It seemed to both of us that to reprint what had been published before was preferable to writing something new, in order to preclude its being supposed that what we said was dictated, or influenced, by the needs of the moment: the three papers express not views framed hastily at the time, but views which had been formed deliberately long before, and held by each of us for many years. We have reason to believe that the papers have been

# PREFACE

appreciated and found useful. Misunderstandings, such as those alluded to, seem, however, unfortunately, to be still prevalent in many quarters; and the three papers have been accordingly reprinted again,—with the addition of a fourth, the second in the present volume, which seemed to us to touch upon some aspects of the subject which ought not to be forgotten,—in the hope that they may still be found useful in removing apprehensions, and in bringing home to our readers both the necessity, and the value, of the study in question.

Our aim in the present Preface is, firstly, to point out a prevalent and serious misconception of the scope of the "Higher Criticism." The word "critic" means *able to distinguish*, and "criticism" means the *power* or *art of distinguishing*. Both terms may, of course, be used of many different kinds of "distinguishing"; but the "higher" criticism—the methods of which are applicable to any ancient writing, and are by no means restricted to the Bible—is so called in contradistinction to the "lower" or textual criticism. When the text of an ancient writing has been settled, as accurately as possible, by the canons of textual criticism, it becomes the province of the "higher" criticism to determine its origin, date, and (if it be composite) literary structure, by "distinguishing" between the *data* available for the purpose. The adjective (the sense of which is often misunderstood) has reference simply to the higher and more

# PREFACE

difficult class of problems, with which, as opposed to textual criticism, the "higher" criticism has to deal. The problems which form the subject of the "Higher Criticism" are thus properly *literary* problems. When the date and historical setting of an ancient writing have been determined, it is no doubt natural to draw inferences as to its credibility and the historical character of the events described in it: but these questions belong properly not to the "higher" criticism, but to *historical* criticism; and to extend the term "Higher Criticism," so as to make it include not only the consideration of such historical problems, but even speculations, probable and improbable alike, on subjects such as the origin of the traditions or civilization of the ancient Hebrews, and the influence of Babylonia upon them, is to abuse it. The proper function of the "Higher Criticism" is to determine the origin, date, and literary structure of an ancient writing: it provides materials for the historical critic, and is thus ancillary to historical criticism, but is itself distinct from it. The confusion is no doubt due to the fact that scholars who are, amongst other things, "higher critics" have also in their writings discussed, and expressed judgments upon, historical problems such as those which have been referred to: but in so far as they have done this, they have done it, not as "higher critics," but as historians or historical critics; and the fact forms no justification for attributing to the "Higher

## PREFACE

Criticism" judgments and conclusions with which it has properly nothing to do.

So much in explanation of the true scope of the "Higher Criticism." Upon other points the papers which follow will speak for themselves. In the first are stated some of the grounds which, as it seems to both of us, make the "Higher Criticism" a necessity at the present day, and give its generally accepted conclusions a pressing claim upon the careful consideration of Christian men. The second discusses further the inevitableness and legitimacy of Criticism. It is shown that the study of the Bible cannot be isolated from the influence of contemporary methods of study and modes of thought; and in particular how modern methods of examining literary and historical documents, and the doctrine of development, compel us to revise many traditional ideas in regard to the Old Testament. The arguments frequently urged against the legitimacy of criticism on the grounds of its novelty and the authority of the New Testament are examined, and its value for the better understanding of the Old Testament is pointed out. In the third some account is given of the changed views which the discoveries and researches of the last half-century have obliged thoughtful men to adopt with regard to the Old Testament, and of the help afforded by the "Higher Criticism" in throwing its different parts into their true historical perspective, and thereby not only bringing out with great vivid-

## PREFACE

ness their historical significance, but also setting before us far more clearly than appeared before the course along which God guided His people Israel, and gradually led them to a fuller knowledge of Himself. In the fourth paper it is shown that the application to the Old Testament of the methods of the "Higher Criticism" implies no denial of its inspiration or disparagement of its contents, but that it must ever remain, in the estimation of Christian men, a living source of moral and religious truth.

Mention has been made above of the "generally accepted" conclusions of the "Higher Criticism"; and a few words may not be out of place in explanation of the expression. Naturally, in a subject covering a wide area, and embracing many and varied details, some conclusions have been drawn which, though they approve themselves to individual critics, rest upon fewer and slighter *data* than others, and are not accepted by all critics; it also happens in this, as in other branches of research, that suggestions and hypotheses are not unfrequently put forth tentatively,—and also usefully, as indicating the lines upon which attention should be directed and investigation carried on,—which do not ultimately receive the approval of critics in general, but prove to be ill-founded or arbitrary; and conclusions of this individual or provisional character are sometimes incorrectly spoken of as though they were the conclusions of higher critics generally. Of course, also,

## PREFACE

the expression does not include the questionable historical speculations which have been recently—though, as has been shown above, unjustly—laid somewhat freely to the charge of the "Higher Criticism." There are also other cases in which it is important to remember that the position of critics is frequently misunderstood by their opponents, who in consequence often urge objections which are, it is true, conclusive against the misapprehended position of critics, but are destitute of all cogency against their *real* position.* It is, indeed, sometimes

* Thus, to take an example of one of the commonest of these misunderstandings, within the last two months critics have been credited, by writers who might have been supposed to be well informed, with maintaining the post-exilic origin of the rites and ceremonies of the priestly law, and even that of "the law" in general, and objections have been urged which would undeniably be fatal to these positions. But as, in point of fact, no critic holds these positions, the real critical position remains obviously unaffected by the objections. What critics really hold is not that the priestly law *originated*, or was "devised," in or after the exile (which would indeed be utterly inconsistent with the known facts), but that, while the chief ceremonial institutions of Israel were *in their origin* of great antiquity, the laws respecting them were gradually developed and elaborated, and that *in the shape in which they are formulated in the priestly sections of the Pentateuch* they belong to the exilic or early post-exilic period. The institutions of the priestly law are thus the final outcome of a long established Temple usage. This position is very different from the belief that these institutions were the "invention" of the exilic or post-exilic period, and is perfectly consistent with all the known facts, even including the injunction to observe the Feast of Unleavened Cakes in 419 B.C., and the mention of the burnt-offering, the meal-offering, and frankincense in 409 B.C., in the papyri discovered recently at Elephantine in Upper Egypt. See further the writer's *Introduction to the Literature of the Old Testament*, p. 142, or his essay on the "Critical Study of the Old Testament," in the series called *Essays for the Times* (Francis Griffiths), No. 21, pp. 30-33.

## PREFACE

asserted that even the most generally accepted conclusions of the "Higher Criticism" are contradicted
by archæology: but our readers must rest assured
that this is not the case: such statements rest
uniformly upon some misapprehension either of the
grounds upon which critics rest their conclusions,
or of the bearing of the facts of archæology upon
them.* It need only be added, lastly, that in what
has been said, both in this Preface and in the
papers which follow,—except in one or two places
where the contrary will be self-evident,—the Old
Testament alone has been held in view. With
regard to the New Testament, it may be sufficient
to observe that, as has been pointed out below
(p. 52), the very different conditions under which
the writings of the New Testament were produced,
and especially the relatively short interval of time
separating them from the period of our Lord's life
upon earth, make it to our minds impossible that
the application to it of the methods of the "Higher
Criticism" (in the legitimate sense of the expression),
though it may alter our view of the origin and structure of some of the documents concerned, should
ever affect appreciably the historical evidence for all
the leading facts of our Lord's life, or for the vital
truths of Christianity.                           S. R. D.

*November* 18, 1911.

* See for illustrations an article by G. B. Gray, in the *Expositor*,
May, 1898, p. 337 ff. ; Hogarth's *Authority and Archæology* (1899),
p. 143 ff.; or Chapman's *Introduction to the Pentateuch* (uniform
with the volumes of the *Cambridge Bible*), 1911, p. 305 ff.

# CONTENTS

# The Claims of Criticism upon the Clergy and Laity.

# THE CLAIMS OF CRITICISM UPON THE CLERGY AND LAITY.*

## By A. F. KIRKPATRICK, D.D.

THE aim of the Christian student is truth; and the aim of the Christian teacher is to bring that truth to bear upon human character and life. The Old Testament forms an integral part of the Bible. It was placed in the hands of the Christian Church by its Founder and His Apostles as the record of God's revelation of Himself to His chosen people and the manifold preparation for His own coming; as the source from which instruction in conduct was to be derived and as the means by which the spiritual life was to be fed. We cannot, therefore, treat it as any other book: it is sacred ground; reverence is demanded of us as we approach it. But it is no true reverence which would exempt it from the fullest examination by all legitimate methods of criticism. Inquiry into the origin, the structure, the character, the meaning of the books which compose it is not only permissible, but indispensable. "To discover more clearly how anything

* A Paper read at the Church Congress, Northampton, October, 1902.

has grown may enable us more truly to estimate its worth and to distinguish it more confidently from all other things." God's revelation of Himself was progressive, and its interpretation must be progressive. We may reasonably expect that "every increase of knowledge will bring forth a deeper knowledge of the truth committed to His Church." New modes of thought, more searching methods of literary and historical investigation, fresh discoveries of science and archæology, must necessarily affect and modify the interpretation of the Bible. It was once as easy as it was natural to regard the first chapter of Genesis as a literal account of the way in which the universe was brought into being; now that we have read the records of the rocks and learnt some fragments of the mystery of the heavens, we know that it cannot be regarded as literal history. But its religious value remains unaltered. It teaches religious truths which geology and astronomy could never teach with authority—truths which are more important for the mass of mankind than all the results of the most elaborate scientific researches.

But truth is not to be won without effort and, it may be, pain; and even, as it may seem, temporary loss. Times of change must be times of trial. They call for faith, courage, patience, sympathy:—for faith that God is still teaching His Church, as He taught it of old, πολυμερῶς καὶ πολυτρόπως, "by divers portions and in divers manners" (Heb. i. 1); for courage to go forward trustfully, following the light of the reason which God has given us; for patience to "prove all things" and "hold fast that which is good"; for sympathy between those who cling to tradition and those who are animated by the desire for progress.

Now, what is the position of students and teachers of the Bible to-day? They are face to face with a treatment of the Bible, especially the Old Testament, which half a century ago would have seemed utterly irreverent, subversive of the foundations of the faith; and which still seems to many (it is not to be wondered at) irreverent and mischievous. Let me try briefly to state what modern criticism is saying with regard to the Old Testament. Pardon me if, for the sake of brevity, my statement is somewhat blunt and dogmatic.

(1) Textual criticism declares the text to be seriously corrupt. The old theory of the perfection of the Massoretic text—*i.e.*, the "traditional" Hebrew text, as fixed and handed down by the later Jewish scribes—is no longer tenable in the face of a mass of cumulative evidence to the contrary.

(2) Linguistic criticism throws doubt upon the interpretation of not a few passages. The meaning of words is disputed; grammatical constructions are ambiguous; allusions are obscure; translation fails adequately to convey the meaning of the original, and honesty compels us to recognize an element of uncertainty in a multitude of renderings.

5

## THE CLAIMS OF CRITICISM

(3) **The** so-called "higher,"* or literary, criticism
has investigated the origin of the various books, and
pronounces that some books once supposed to have
been written by single authors are compilations with
a long and complicated literary history, and that
some books cannot have been written by the authors
whose names they bear. Sometimes it goes further,
and asserts that some books have been revised and
interpolated in such a way that their original authors
would hardly be able to recognize them.

(4) Historical criticism affirms that much of the
history has been coloured by the beliefs and practices
of the times in which the books were compiled, long
after the events, and must be regarded as rather an
ideal than an actual picture of the national life. It
requires us to a great extent to revolutionize our
views of the course of the history of Israel.

(5) The researches of archæology and the com-
parative study of religions show that the religion of
Israel derived many elements from the primitive
religion of the Semites, possessed much in common
with the religions of surrounding nations, and was
largely influenced in its development by the faiths
with which it came in contact in the course of its
history.

In these and other ways modern criticism is de-
manding a new treatment of the Bible, which seems

* On the meaning of this expression, see the Preface to the
present pamphlet, pp. vi-viii.

to many incompatible with the reverence due to it; it is offering a new view of the Bible which seems to many to impair, if not to destroy its value. Is not all this perplexing, disquieting, unsettling? Yes; but the new movement cannot be ignored; it cannot be crushed by denunciation; if it rests, as its advocates claim that it does, upon the honest recognition of facts, it must in the end be triumphant. Now practically every one who has made any serious study of the Old Testament has felt himself compelled to admit that the traditional view of its character— the view which was generally accepted fifty years ago—can no longer be maintained without modification. Many students of the Old Testament, probably a majority of them, have found themselves compelled to go further, to accept critical principles, and to revise their views of its textual, literary, and historical character to a greater or less degree, in the directions I have indicated. They have done so, not in obedience to any à priori philosophical or theological theories, but as the result of a careful and unprejudiced examination of the facts in the light of modern critical methods and enlarged knowledge. But they have not abandoned their belief that the Old Testament is the God-given record of God's special revelation of Himself through Israel in preparation for the Incarnation, and as such of permanent significance for the Christian Church.

This being the case, the clergy are in duty bound

to endeavour to understand the methods of criticism, to estimate the validity of its results, and to consider how those results, if true, must affect their teaching. For if those methods are, generally speaking, sound; if those results are, to any considerable extent, valid; readers of the Bible must be gently and gradually prepared to accept them. The responsibility laid upon the teachers of the present generation is to guide those entrusted to their care safely through the inevitable dangers of a time of change; to show that the Bible is not less the Word of God because we are forced, in the light of modern research, to acknowledge that it does not possess many characteristics which it was once believed to possess, and which had come to be regarded as essential notes of a record of divine revelation; to explain how its religious value is not diminished, but increased, by a courageous treatment of it in the light of fuller knowledge. The clergy who are to teach must teach themselves; they have promised to be diligent in such studies as help to the knowledge of Holy Scripture; and some knowledge of modern criticism is indispensable, partly that they may avoid basing the truth of Christianity upon insecure foundations and defending positions which they will presently be forced to abandon; partly that they may not be guilty of ignoring the new light upon the meaning of Scripture which God intends should be thrown by the progress of modern thought. For there is a grave danger to faith in insisting upon views which the majority of thinking men have found or will shortly find to be untenable; and there is a serious loss to the faith if the results of criticism are ignored, supposing its claim to offer a larger and sounder theology is to any extent well-grounded. I do not plead that the processes or results of modern criticism should often, if ever, be directly discussed in the pulpit; in many churches they would be utterly out of place and would only perplex and annoy; but I do believe that they must be taken careful account of in determining the way in which the Old Testament is taught, if the faith of the next generation is to be spared an abrupt and perilous shock.

But here it is necessary, in view of certain recent developments of criticism, to point out that it is all-important to distinguish between sober criticism, the results of which have been tested and are generally accepted, and speculative criticism, which is the outcome of individual ingenuity, and is never likely to command a general approval. Sober criticism is objective; it carefully collects facts, arranges them, and endeavours to ascertain their meaning. It recognizes its limitations; it acknowledges that many of its conclusions are only probable. Speculative criticism is subjective; it often pretends to impossibilities; it depends on the intuition of the critic; and frequently it convinces no one but himself. Thus, for example, it must be admitted that in a

# THE CLAIMS OF CRITICISM

large number of instances the text of the Old Testament is corrupt, and honesty requires us to acknowledge it; but it is absurd to suppose that in more than a few instances the original text can with certainty be restored by conjecture; and it is ridiculous to imagine that history can be re-written by the aid of a long series of unsupported guesses, however ingenious. The results of literary criticism are at best only probable, though in many cases the probability amounts to practical certainty; but literary criticism has been pushed to the wildest extremes, as for instance when we are told that we have no genuine writings of the prophet Jeremiah except a few lyric poems, and that only a dim remembrance of the grand form of the prophet is to be discerned in the poetic portions of the book. The results of historical criticism, again, are only probable; it may easily be mistaken in its attempts to reconstruct history from scanty details; it is often presumptuous in presenting as certainties what are only tentative theories. Every movement is sure to have its extravagances; they misrepresent and injure it, for those who dislike the movement are only too ready to judge it by its extravagances, and to point to them as characteristic, when they are mere excrescences; and at the present time there are such extravagances of criticism, which must not be regarded as normal and representative. Those on whom lies the responsibility of teaching are bound to examine and discriminate.

But to return to our main subject. In what ways does modern criticism affect theology, i.e., our whole view of the content of God's revelation of Himself and of the way in which it was given and recorded ? Let me speak of three points—the mode of revelation, the character of prophecy, the nature of inspiration.

(1) It leads us to regard God's revelation of Himself as a more gradual process than we had supposed it to be; effected to a large extent by the action of ordinary forces, developed in ways which we should now call natural rather than supernatural. There is an analogy between the process of revelation and the process of creation as we now understand it. The shaping of the universe, we now know, was the work not of six literal days, but of immeasurable ages; yet it was no whit the less the obedient response of matter to the fiat of Omnipotence. The lofty creed of ethical Monotheism was not flashed into the heart of the nation once for all amid the lightnings of Sinai, but won through many a struggle and many a failure; yet none the less it was Jehovah's message to the nation from the day when He brought it out of the land of Egypt.

(2) Prophecy, that unique gift of ancient Israel, was far more closely linked with the time and circumstances of its delivery than was formerly thought. We should place its evidential value now far more in its moral force than in its predictions, though this element must not be denied or minimised. It was

11

the exposition of eternal principles in the language of the time; rooted in the history and institutions of the chosen people; conditioned by the temperaments and fortunes and environments of individual prophets; yet none the less surely a message from God, and no mere fanciful aspiration of enthusiasts and fanatics, or natural expression of moral ideals by the best representatives of a naturally religious race.

(3) Criticism compels us to revise our doctrine of the inspiration of Scripture. We must not ascribe an equal value and authority to every part of the Old Testament. We must no longer talk of its infallibility and inerrancy. We must distinguish its temporary, imperfect elements. Our Lord Himself taught us to do so. While we hold fast to the belief that the Old Testament contains the record—the divinely-shaped record—of God's revelation of Himself to Israel and through Israel, we seem to be forced to admit that the record was not given and has not been preserved in such form as we might antecedently have expected and as has generally been believed. And surely, in this connexion, the fact that for centuries the Old Testament was known to the Church only through most imperfect versions gives much matter for reflection.

What follows from these results of criticism? Is not our theology liberated, deepened, strengthened?

(1) It is liberated.—We are relieved of a multitude of difficulties in the study of the Old Testament

when we accept in general principle, if not in every detail, the critical account of its origin and character. We need no longer spend our time and energy in attempting to reconcile every supposed discrepancy. We can recognize most frankly that the immoralities and barbarities and imprecations which shock us belong to a lower stage of religious history. Unfulfilled prophecies need no longer perplex us. We can look away from details to the great central truths which were being slowly taught to an unwilling nation, to the great divine purpose for the world which was being patiently wrought out in and through the vicissitudes of the nation's history and the sufferings and triumphs of its individual members.

(2) It is deepened.—For at the present moment, through the instrumentality of this criticism, which to many seems destructive and unsettling, God is surely driving us back, lovingly if sternly, from the letter to the spirit; from the word to the Speaker; from external details to the great spiritual truths which underlie them. We only follow our Lord's example if we concentrate attention on the great principles which sum up the teaching of the Old Testament (Matt. vii. 12; xxii. 40).

(3) It is strengthened.—Criticism compels us to a deeper and more careful study of the way in which God wrought out His purposes in the world in history as well as in creation; and I cannot but believe

13

that it has a special message for our time, because it presents to us a view of His action in past history which will confirm our faith and help us to believe more confidently in His continued working in the world. As we enter more and more sympathetically into the nature of the process of God's working in old time we begin to realize how hard it must have been at the time to be sure that God was guiding the destinies of Israel; yet as we survey the completed history we cannot fail to trace His guidance: and so we are encouraged to believe that, hard as we may sometimes find it to recognize His guiding hand in the tangled history of the present, all is converging to the "one far-off divine event"—the universal establishment of His eternal sovereignty.

# THE INEVITABLENESS AND LEGITIMACY
## OF CRITICISM.

## II.

## THE INEVITABLENESS AND LEGITIMACY OF CRITICISM.*

I.—Each age has its trials of faith which come to it through the progress of thought and the advance of knowledge. Upon each successive generation is laid the task of adapting its interpretation of the Bible to the growing knowledge of the time; and in an age when new methods of investigation and new modes of thought are affecting all our studies, changes, and startling changes, are inevitable in regard to our conceptions of the character of the Bible. Loyalty to fresh light is not less a duty than loyalty to our inheritance from the past. The education of the world goes on apace, and unless Theology can keep in touch with it, it must renounce its claim to be the Queen of Sciences. And then religion must inevitably suffer. Forcible repression of freedom of thought must foster superstition or scepticism, and in the end it is compelled to acknowledge its defeat. The study of the Bible cannot be isolated from the influence of contemporary methods of study and modes of thought.

* A Paper read at the St. Albans Diocesan Conference, October, 1904, and reprinted from the *Interpreter* for March, 1905, p. 201 *ff*.

History abounds in warnings. "Luther denounced Copernicus as an arrogant foe who wrote in defiance of Scripture, and Melanchthon urged the suppression of such mischievous doctrines by the secular power."* The terrors of the Inquisition were invoked to silence Galileo. But Astronomy triumphed. Not half a century ago Geology was supposed to be antagonistic to religion, and it is only by slow degrees that we have come to see that Scripture and Science cannot be at variance, because Scripture was never intended to teach Science, and must be interpreted in accordance with the established results of Science. We can now listen with equanimity to a science which postulates enormous periods for the development of the earth, and thinks that man may have existed on it for 50,000 or even 100,000 years.

II.—There are two forces at work in the present day, compelling us to revise many of our traditional ideas with regard to the Old Testament: (a) the modern methods of examining historical and literary documents; (b) the doctrine of development. Shall we attempt to crush them by denunciation? If the methods of investigation and the principles of thought are sound and scientific, the attempt, as experience shews, is foredoomed to failure. Let me quote the opinion of an eminent historian in regard to them, and first, in regard to the examination of documents. In his inaugural lecture, Professor Bury,

* Chambers' Encyclopædia, iii., 462.

# LEGITIMACY OF CRITICISM

Lord Acton's successor in the Chair of Modern History at Cambridge, spoke of "the revolution which is slowly and silently progressing" in historical studies. Before the beginning of the last century the study of history was, as a rule, not scientific. But "erudition has now been supplanted by scientific method." It was "not a historian but a philologist," who "gave a powerful stimulus to the introduction of critical methods which are now universally applied. Six years before the eighteenth century closed a modest book appeared at Halle, of which it is perhaps hardly a grave exaggeration to say that it is one of half a dozen which in the last three hundred years have exercised most effective influence upon thought. The work I mean is Wolf's *Prolegomena to Homer.* It launched upon the world a new engine —*donum exitiale Minervae*—which was soon to menace the walls of many a secure citadel. It gave historians the idea of a systematic and minute method of analysing their sources, which soon developed into the microscopic criticism, now recognised as indispensable."

Let me call another witness in the same department of study. In his excellent handbook on *The Study of Ecclesiastical History* the late Bishop of Gibraltar, Dr. Collins, writes, (p. 33), "The next step that the student must undertake is the *examination of the documents* which he has obtained. He must take them one by one and examine and appraise

19

them as carefully as he can. Is this a faithful text or is it corrupt ? is it really the work of the author to whom it is ascribed ? was he a contemporary witness ? if not, when did he live ? when did he write ? what were his opportunities of knowing the facts ? was he biassed, and if so, in what direction ? did he write with a purpose, and if so, with what purpose ? What can be learned on these points from internal, and what from external evidence ? and do the conclusions agree to which these two respectively lead ? Such are the questions which must be asked with regard to each document; and the answers to these questions, so far as they can be ascertained, must henceforward be borne constantly in mind in dealing with the documents concerned."

These methods have been applied to the books of the Bible, and these questions have inevitably been asked concerning them. We cannot isolate the study of the Bible, and refuse to submit it to the processes which are freely applied to all literature and all historical documents. Its sacred character cannot exempt it from such inquiries. We believe it to be inspired; but we have no right to assume *a priori* that inspiration would render such investigations superfluous or profane: and the most elementary acquaintance with a few simple facts shews the untenableness of such an assumption.

We can no longer approach the study of the Old Testament with a belief in the absolute integrity of

20

the text. In the seventeenth century there were scholars who went so far as to maintain the inspiration and absolute accuracy of even the vowel points of the Massoretic Text, but the simplest application of the principles of textual criticism demonstrates the impossibility of such a hypothesis. There are traditions of date and authorship received from the Jewish Church and long regarded as authoritative, which can no longer be upheld, when they are tested by internal evidence. Books and groups of books supposed to have been written by a single author are seen to be compilations from sources differing widely in character; and some books contain the plainest indications of a date at variance with the traditional attribution. If two accounts of the same event are inconsistent, we are compelled to endeavour to form a judgment which is the most trustworthy, and to explain how the discrepancy is to be accounted for.

Whatever difficulties may be raised, these questions must be investigated patiently, thoroughly, dispassionately. We must not be alarmed if we find the same phenomena meeting us in our sacred documents which we find in secular writings. In so far as the cases are parallel, they must be dealt with in the same way.

III.—Let us take a simple illustration of the compilatory character of the historical books. In chapters vii. to xii. of the First Book of Samuel two independent accounts of the election of Saul to be king are combined. One is contained in chapters ix., x. 1-16, xi.: the other in chapters vii., viii., x. 17-27, xii. In the first, Samuel appears as a seer who may be consulted for advice in cases of difficulty, but famous apparently only in his own neighbourhood. In the second, Samuel is the Judge of Israel, who goes on circuit from place to place over a considerable district. According to the first account, Israel is oppressed by the Philistines; their cry has come up to Jehovah, and He has determined to send them a deliverer. According to the second, the Philistines have been repulsed by the Israelites under Samuel's leadership; the demand for a king comes from the people, who are discontented with the misgovernment of Samuel's sons; and it is condemned as a wicked rejection of Jehovah's sovereignty. According to the first account, Saul is brought to Samuel by a chain of providential circumstances, privately anointed by him, and directed to await his opportunity, which comes shortly afterwards when the men of Jabesh send round to their countrymen in the hope of finding allies to save them from the brutality of Nahash. According to the second account, Saul is chosen by lot in a public assembly of the nation at Mizpah, and takes over the government when Samuel lays down his office in a touching farewell address to the people.

Now in the light of modern principles of discrim-

ination of sources, it is clear that we have here two
different accounts of the establishment .of the monarchy, derived from different sources and pieced
together by a compiler, who, according to the method
of Oriental historiographers and mediæval chron-
iclers, compiled his history by combining the documents or traditions to which he had access, instead
of digesting their contents, and writing an entirely
fresh narrative. He does not study logical consist-
ency, or attempt to remove the discrepancies, save
by some few editorial additions, which serve to
some extent to unite the narratives and to conceal
their mutual inconsistency. We may attempt to
reconcile the narratives; it is possible that if we had
all the facts before us we could do so: but is it not
better frankly to acknowledge that we have here two
accounts of the establishment of the monarchy,
written from different points of view ? The first
account gives an ancient tradition of the origin of
the monarchy in the urgent need of Israel for a
deliverer. From one point of view the monarchy
was necessary, in order to weld the tribes together
and enable them to shew a united front to their
enemies. In view of the actual circumstances of the
nation, it was God's will that Israel should have a
king. The second account contains a later prophetic
reflection on the establishment of the monarchy.
From another point of view it was wrong for Israel
to wish for a king. It was a declension from the

ideal of theocracy, the direct government of the nation by Jehovah. This reflection, instead of being thrown into the form of an abstract discussion, was expressed in the concrete form of a historical narrative. The compiler combined the two narratives, leaving his readers to draw the lessons. On the one hand the establishment of the monarchy was an evidence of God's care for his people. Saul was divinely raised up and divinely appointed. On the other hand the desire of the Israelites for a king "that they might be like other nations" was an indication of distrust of God and failure to rise to the height of their peculiar position as a nation distinct from the nations of the world. Each of the accounts presents an idea which it is important we should grasp in order to have a true view of the course and meaning of the history of Israel. It may be that the first and older narrative is true historically in the narrower sense of agreement with the facts as they actually happened; while the second and later narrative is equally true historically in the wider sense of a true comment on the facts in the light of the ideal Divine purpose. That the ideal as well as the actual should be expressed in the form of a narrative is due to the "realising" genius of the Hebrew mind, I mean its tendency to embody ideas in a concrete historical form.

IV.—Literary traditions must be tested by internal evidence, and if internal evidence clearly contradicts

the traditions of an uncritical age, they must give
way before it. The most obvious instance is the
later part of the Book of Isaiah. If Isaiah xl. to
xlviii. (I do not include chapters xlix. to lxvi. because
they present greater difficulties) had come down to
us as a detached and anonymous prophecy, we could
have had no hesitation in dating it in the closing
years of the Babylonian Exile, when Cyrus had
already embarked on his career of conquest, but
before Babylon had opened its gates to him. Internal evidence is often precarious and inconclusive,
but in this particular case the cumulative weight of
the arguments from historical allusions, literary style,
and theological contents, tells irresistibly against the
authorship and age of Isaiah, and in favour of the
age of the Exile. The significance of the prophecy
gains enormously by the transference, and our knowledge of the circumstances of the exiles is largely
extended.

V.—There are two arguments urged against the
legitimacy and the validity of criticism, about which I
wish to say a few words. They are the arguments of
(a) novelty, and (b) authority.

(a) It is not uncommonly urged that critical views
of the Old Testament are untrustworthy, because
they are new. They are spoken of as "unproved
hypotheses, resting on no further proof than was
available to all the scholars of the past nineteen
centuries." The argument is one which would con-

demn all progress. Why was not the heliocentric theory of the solar system discovered before Copernicus ? Why had so many great discoveries and inventions to wait till the nineteenth century ? Were not human brains as fertile in earlier ages ? But here is what a recognised authority on the study of History tells us :—

"Many centuries and whole eras of brilliant civilisation had to pass away before the first dawn of criticism was visible among the most intellectual peoples in the world. Neither the Orientals nor the Middle Ages ever formed a definite conception of it. Up to our own day there have been enlightened men who, in employing documents for the purpose of writing history, have neglected the most elementary precautions, and unconsciously assumed false generalisations . . . For criticism is antagonistic to the normal bent of the mind."* The critical spirit is, you see, a modern instrument even in its application to history generally. But further it must be remembered that until quite recent times the study of the Bible has been pursued under the domination of a rigid theory of verbal inspiration. It is only within the last forty or fifty years that we have broken loose from its trammels, and realised that it is inconsistent with facts, and that the truth of the Gospel is not dependent upon it.

* Langlois and Seignobos, *Introduction to the Study of History*, p. 68.

(*b*) A second and more serious argument against the legitimacy of criticism is that of the authority of the New Testament. Our Lord Himself, it is urged, sanctioned what may be called the "traditional" view of the Old Testament, and by implication at any rate, condemned the critical view. I fully recognise that here we enter on difficult and delicate ground. I have the greatest respect for those who shrink from anything which seems to detract from our Lord's authority. But in condescending to become incarnate as a Jew at a particular epoch in a particular country our Lord necessarily accepted conditions and limitations of time and place. Doubtless in virtue of the universality of His humanity He transcended those conditions so that He is equally in sympathy with every age and every race. But He must speak and teach in Aramaic, the vernacular of Palestine.* He must use the terminology of the time in regard to physical phenomena. Must He not have used it also in regard to the Old Testament? The questions which are raised by modern criticism were not before Him, any more than the questions which are raised by modern science.

I would ask anyone who feels the difficulty, to examine very carefully what is the nature and extent of the New Testament use and endorsement of the Old Testament. What is it that our Lord and His Apostles guarantee? Our Lord certainly taught that

* See Hastings' *Dictionary of the Bible*, v., p. 5.

the Old Testament Scriptures in their threefold division of Law, Prophets, and Writings, testified of Him. By their use of the Old Testament Scriptures, not less than by actual statement, the Apostles shewed that they believed them to be profitable for doctrine, for reproof, for instruction in righteousness. But the freedom with which they quoted them, and the simple fact that they generally made use of the Septuagint Version, shew that it is the general spirit and drift of the teaching of the Old Testament which is endorsed, and not every fact or statement therein contained. No one would now maintain that because Evangelists and Apostles for the most part use the Septuagint they therefore endorse all the blunders of that Version. While I believe most firmly that the New Testament recognises the Old Testament as "an essential part of the Christian Bible," I cannot believe that its interpretation is to be limited by what was known or was possible in the Apostolic age.

VI. I can only speak most briefly of the second force which I mentioned as affecting our study of the Old Testament,—the doctrine of development. "The world is not yet alive," writes Prof. Bury in the Inaugural Lecture (p. 19) to which I have already referred, "to the full importance of the transformation of history (as part of a wider transformation) which is being brought about by the doctrine of development." Nowhere, perhaps, has this idea of gradual, orderly development, of continuous evolution, had more influence than in remodelling our conceptions of the course of Old Testament history and the growth of Old Testament religion. But it may be urged that the acknowledgment of evolution in the history of the Old Testament leads to mere natural-ism, and the denial of the reality of revelation. "Is the ethical code of the Bible complete and final and perfect ?" asks Blatchford in *God and my Neighbour* (p. 19). "No. The ethical code of the Bible gradually developes and improves. Had it been divine it would have been perfect from the first. It is because it **is human that it** developes. As the prophets and the poets of the Jews grew wiser and gentler and more enlightened, so the revelation of God grew wiser and gentler with them. Now, God would know from the beginning; but men would have to learn. Therefore the Bible writings would appear to be human and not divine." Such language sounds plausible perhaps to the class to which it is addressed. I pass over the astounding assumptions upon which it is based. But when we look at the history of that evolution, and mark how religion progressed by and in spite of a constant conflict between the higher and lower ten-dencies in the nation, we are compelled to ask, What was the power that taught Israel ? What made Israel differ from surrounding nations closely related to it, and speaking almost an identical language ? What kept Israel from being absorbed by the Canaanites, who were superior to them in strength, and more advanced in civilisation ? The Christian answer is the true one :—that the progress recorded in the Old Testament is not merely an inevitable evolution of human thought, a natural advance in knowledge and morality, but an evolution of human thought and an advance in knowledge and morality under the constraint of a divine discipline and the education of a progressive revelation. The claim of the leaders and prophets of Israel to be representatives and spokesmen of God was not baseless. It is attested by the results which culminate in the Incarnation and Christianity.

VII. Critical methods are a means, not an end. Their object is to provide the material for rightly understanding documents, for constructing history and formulating theology. The restoration of texts, the determination of their dates, and the analysis of their sources, are not the final object of the student's labour. It is useful work, it is attractive work, but it is not the highest work. What we want to know is by what steps and in what way God revealed His will to ancient Israel, prepared the way for the Incarnation, laid deeply and surely the foundations upon which the Catholic Church was to be built. The more difficult task of synthesis and interpretation is the real aim of the historian and the theologian.

Again, it is doubtless easy to exaggerate the application of the principle of development. The late

## LEGITIMACY OF CRITICISM

Dr. A. B. Davidson was a master of Old Testament Theology, and this is what his friend and editor, Dr. Salmond, gives as his opinion:—

"He had an increasing distrust of ambitious attempts to fix the date of every separate piece of the Hebrew literature, and link the ideas in their several measures of immaturity and maturity with the writings as thus arranged. He became more and more convinced that there was no solid basis for such confident chronological dispositions of the writings and juxtapositions of the beliefs. In his judgment the only result of endeavours of this kind was to give an entirely fictitious view of the ideas, in their relative degrees of definiteness, the times at which they emerged or came to certainty, and the causes that worked to their origin and development. The most that we had scientific warrant to do, in view of the materials available for the purpose, was, in his opinion, to take the history in large tracts and the literature in a few broad divisions, and study the beliefs and the deliverances in connexion with them."*

VIII.    Dr. Davidson's words lead up to the thoughts with which I wish to conclude. On the one hand, it must never be forgotten that the Old Testament as it stands was the Apostolic Bible,

* Preface to Professor Davidson's *Theology of the Old Testament* (1904), p. vi. It must, however, be remembered that Professor Davidson fully accepted the main conclusions of criticism. See pp. 15 *ff.* of the same volume.

which is commended to us for our study. I accept it as "inspired," though I do not venture to define the nature and limits of inspiration. I am content to believe that the composition, editing, and collection of the books which it contains were divinely controlled in order to adapt it for its purpose, to shew us God working in the world, to furnish spiritual light and comfort to the Church for all time.

On the other hand I cannot doubt that the Old Testament must be interpreted in successive ages by the help of all new light and knowledge which God gives mankind. The great fundamental truths remain the same: our comprehension of the stages and methods by which God revealed them may change. Criticism may enable us to understand the stages of revelation better, to trace the growth of religious thought more exactly, but the great truths are the really important matter. The light and heat and attraction of the sun are facts, independent of theories as to the origin and composition of the sun and the action of gravitation. Only the truths must not be affirmed or expounded in such a way as to contradict what criticism can demonstrate with a reasonable degree of probability.

The critic no doubt often forgets the true purpose of the Old Testament, and the authority by which it has been accredited to us. The anti-critic on the other hand too often assumes that the Bible is what it never claims to be, infallibly accurate in all matters of fact and science. He will have all or nothing. I tremble when I read such words as these: "If the Gospels are not inspired in the strictest sense in which theologians speak of inspiration, these records [viz., of our Lord's discourses] are worthless;"* or when I find defenders of the faith making the perilous assumption that we must proceed on the old traditional lines, or else abandon the foundations of the Gospel and the sanction of its message for the redemption of mankind.

Courage, not cowardice, is the true child of faith; boldness, not bigotry, is the best bulwark of the truth.

* Anderson, *The Bible and Modern Criticism*, p. 18.

# THE OLD TESTAMENT IN THE LIGHT OF TO-DAY.

III.

# THE OLD TESTAMENT IN THE LIGHT OF TO-DAY.*

THE subject on which I propose to speak to-night is "The Old Testament in the Light of To-day." The subject is a wide one, and there are aspects of it on which naturally I can only touch in passing, or which I may even have to pass by altogether; but it seemed to me to be one that would embrace points of view which might be suitably considered upon an occasion which suggested rather naturally a comparison of the present with the past. We are standing at the end of a century which has been marked, almost more than any other, by a great intellectual awakening, and which certainly more than any other has been fruitful in great discoveries. Sciences which a hundred years ago were practically non-existent have now arrived at a vigorous and independent manhood; the observation of nature in all its departments has been pursued with indefatigable industry and skill, and lines of investigation, once unworked, have been opened up, and have been found

* An address delivered in connection with the Jubilee of the New College, Hampstead, on Wednesday, November 7, 1900; and reprinted here from the *Expositor*, January, 1901, p. 27 ff.

often to conduct to startling and unexpected results. And the methods which in all these studies have been productive of solid results have been these—the systematic and all-sided observation of facts, the shrinking from no labour or pains to solve a difficulty or account for what was not fully understood, the bringing to bear upon a new subject whatever light or illustration might be available from other quarters, the endeavour to correlate, and subsume under general laws, the new facts discovered. Advance conducted upon lines such as these has been most marked throughout the century. It may have been most conspicuous and brilliant in the physical sciences and in the great mechanical arts based upon them; but it has been not less real in many other branches of knowledge, in language, in history, in archæology, in anthropology. How much, in all these departments of knowledge, is known now, which a century ago was unknown, and even unsuspected! How much more familiar are we now, for instance, not only with the languages, but also with the habits and institutions, and art of the Greeks and Romans! How many dark points in their history and antiquities have been cleared up by the numerous inscriptions that have been found and published during recent years! Even since these last lines were written* news has arrived of remarkable discoveries at Cnossus, in Crete, which promise in some respects

*In 1900.

to revolutionize former ideas of the early character and history of Greek civilization. On these and other subjects we owe our enlarged knowledge, partly to the discovery of new materials, partly to the application to old materials of more exact and systematic methods of inquiry. The facts of nature lay before our forefathers as fully as they lie before ourselves; yet how strangely they failed to elicit from them the secrets hidden within them! The great masterpieces of Greek literature were all familiar to the scholars of the sixteenth century; and yet some of the most serious blots on the Authorized Version of the New Testament are due to the translators' ignorance of some quite elementary principles of Greek syntax!* But the same spirit of scientific study and research which has inspired new life into so many other departments of knowledge, and even in some instances created them altogether, has also pervaded Biblical and Oriental learning; and there is hardly any branch of these subjects, whether language, or literature, or antiquities, or history, in which the stimulus of the nineteenth century has not made itself felt, and in which improved methods of investigation have not conducted to new and important results.

I may assume on the part of those who hear me a

* See, for illustrations, Professor (afterwards Bishop) Lightfoot's illuminative volume *On a Fresh Revision of the English New Testament*—a book which, though published in 1871, is still full of instruction, and in no respect antiquated.

general familiarity with the new light in which, to those who do not refuse to open their eyes, the Old Testament appears to-day. The historical books are now seen to be not, as was once supposed, the works (for instance) of Moses, or Joshua, or Samuel. They are seen to present a multiplicity of phenomena which cannot be accounted for, or reasonably explained, except upon the supposition that they came into existence gradually; that they are compiled out of the writings of distinct and independent authors, characterized by different styles and representing different points of view, which were combined together and otherwise adjusted, till they finally assumed their present form. The various documents thus brought to light reveal, further, such mutual differences that in many cases they can no longer be held to be the work of contemporary writers, or to spring, as used to be thought, from a single generation: in the Pentateuch, especially, the groups of laws contained in the different strata of narrative differ in such a way that they can only be supposed to have been codified at widely different periods of the national life, to the history and literature of which they correspond, and the principles dominant in which they accurately reflect. Three well-defined stages in literature, legislation, and history thus disclose themselves. Nor is this all. Archæology and anthropology, two sciences which seventy years ago were completely in their in-

fancy, come to our aid, and cast upon the Biblical
history illuminative side-lights. Some progress had
indeed been made seventy years ago in unravelling
from the hieroglyphics the history and antiquities of
ancient Egypt; but the cuneiform records of Babylonia and Assyria refused still to yield up their
secrets. But Edward Hincks had already taken some
important steps towards their decipherment; and
Henry Layard's *Nineveh and its Remains*, which
appeared in 1849, and excited at once the liveliest
interest, told eloquently of a magnificent and imposing civilization which, though as yet all but silent,
was destined before long to be again vocal. Major
(afterwards Sir Henry) Rawlinson's great discoveries
speedily followed; and from 1851 to the present day
the stream of light which has poured from the
mounds of Babylonia and Assyria upon the Eastern
world has flowed unintermittently. The history and
antiquities of two great civilizations, each, in a
different way, having interesting links of connexion
with Israel, are now revealed to us—not, certainly,
in their completeness; for that we must wait still for
many years to come—but, nevertheless, in sufficient
measure to enable us to estimate without serious
error their magnitude and character, and to understand the nature of the influence exerted by them
upon Israel. If not, on the whole, so epoch-making
and surprising in their results as these two splendid
achievements of modern genius and industry, the dis-

covery and publication of inscriptions from Phœnicia, Syria, Moab, and Arabia, and the observations of travellers and explorers in the same regions, have in many important details augmented our former knowledge of the customs, and institutions, and habits of thought of Israel's neighbours, helping us thereby to realize more accurately the position taken by Israel amongst them, and the affinities, mental not less than physical and material, subsisting between them. The net result of these discoveries is that the ancient Hebrews are taken out of the isolation in which, as a nation, they formerly seemed to stand; and it is seen now that many of their institutions and beliefs were not peculiar to themselves; they existed in more or less similar form among their neighbours; they were only in Israel developed in special directions, subordinated to special ends, and made the vehicle of special ideas.*

Archæology has also often a more direct bearing upon the Old Testament: it has made a series of most valuable additions to our knowledge, some-

* In support of the statements in the preceding paragraph, the writer may be permitted to refer to his essay, illustrative of the light shed by archæology upon the Old Testament, in Hogarth's *Authority and Archæology* (1899), pp. 1-152. The code of Hammurabi, king of Babylon,—most probably about 2131-2088 B.C.—had not been discovered when this essay was written; but the general conclusions expressed in the essay are not affected by it. On the early history of the decipherment of the cuneiform inscriptions of Babylonia and Assyria, see the present writer's "Schweich Lectures" on *Modern Research as illustrating the Bible* (1909), pp. 4-7. Lectures II. and III. in this volume

times supporting, sometimes correcting, sometimes supplementing, the Biblical data. What, for instance, can be more stimulating and welcome to the student than the Moabite king's own detailed account of an event dismissed in a single verse in the Kings? or the Assyrian king's own narrative of the entire campaign in which the Rabshakeh's mission to Jerusalem forms, as we now understand, a single episode? or the particulars, recounted by a contemporary, if not by an eye-witness, of Cyrus' conquest of Babylon?* The importance to Biblical history of newly-recovered facts such as these I cannot now pause to develop: I will merely, before I pass on, remind you of the very important light which has been thrown by archæology upon the early chapters of Genesis. The monuments of Egypt and Babylon combine to establish the presence of man upon the earth, and the existence of entirely distinct languages, at periods considerably more ancient than is allowed for by the figures in the Book of Genesis; and the tablets brought from the library of Asshurbanipal have disclosed to us the source of the

contain an account of the light thrown upon Canaan by recent excavations, especially those at Gezer.

On the code of Hammurabi, see, briefly, p. 20 f. in these lectures; more fully Johns, in Hastings' *Dictionary of the Bible*, vol. v., pp. 584-612 (including a translation of the entire code); also, in its bearing on early Hebrew law, the present writer's *Exodus* (in the *Cambridge Bible for Schools and Colleges*), pp. 205, 418 ff.

* See Hogarth, *op. cit.*, pp. 89-90, 105-107, 124-5, 128.

material elements upon which the Biblical narratives of the Creation and the Deluge have been con‑ structed.* A clearer indication that in the early chapters of Genesis we are not reading literal his‑ tory could hardly be found; and we see archæology supporting criticism in pressing upon theologians and apologists the urgent need of a revision of cur‑ rent opinions respecting parts of the Old Testament narrative.

If we turn to the prophets and poetical books, we find, similarly, that they also have in many respects received new light from the studies of the past cen‑ tury. Prophecy is no longer defined, as it was once by a celebrated and still justly honoured divine, as "the history of events before they come to pass."†

* Cf. Dr. F. Watson, at the Church Congress, held in 1900 at Newcastle : the material elements in the Creation-narrative were derived from " ancient traditions, not the peculiar treasure of the chosen people, but traditions current amongst the nations in that plain of Babylonia, which the Bible describes as the aboriginal home of the human race " (*Report of the Newcastle Congress*, p. 153). See for details the articles " Cosmogony," by Principal Whitehouse, and " Flood," by the Rev. F. H. Woods, in Hastings' *Dictionary of the Bible ;* Ball's *Light from the East,* pp. 1-15, 34-41 ; *Authority and Archæology,* pp. 9-27, 32-34 ; or the present writer's *Book of Genesis* (ed. 8, 1911), pp. 27 ff., 103 ff.

† Butler's *Analogy,* part ii., chap. vii., § 3, 6th paragraph. See for the correction of this definition Kirkpatrick's *Doctrine of the Prophets,* ch. i., esp. p. 15 f. There is often a large poetical, or imaginative, element in the prophecy, to which nothing corre‑ sponds in the fulfilment, the fulfilment being limited to the substance of the prophecy,—whether, as the case may be, this is spiritual (*e.g.,* Is. ii. 2, 3), or material (*e.g.,* Is. x. 33, 34 ; xxx. 32, 33). See the writer's *Isaiah, his Life and Times,* in the " Men of the Bible" series, pp. 61, 73, 94-5, 106, 111-14, 146 *note,* 167.

# THE LIGHT OF TO-DAY

More careful and exact exegesis, a truer appreciation
of the aim and object set by the prophet to himself,
the study of his writings in the light of history,
especially with the help of the new materials afforded
by the inscriptions of Assyria and Babylonia, have
shown what the prophets primarily were: they were
primarily the teachers of their own generation: they
spoke out of the circumstances of their own age; it
was the political mistakes, the social abuses, the
moral shortcomings of their own contemporaries
which it was their primary object to correct; their
predictions of national deliverance or disaster, their
broader ideal delineations of a future age of moral
and material blessedness, all start from their own
present, and are conditioned by the historical en-
vironment in which they moved. Nor does their
theological teaching stand all upon the same plane.
It is adapted to the spiritual capacities of those to
whom it is addressed; a progress is in many cases
discernible in it; and the rise and development of
new truths can be traced in their writings.

*Mutatis mutandis*, what has been said holds good
of the poetical books. Their connexion with the
names with which they are traditionally associated
must be almost uniformly abandoned; in some cases
language, in others contents and character, impera-
tively demand this. The poetical books are seen
now in fact to have a much wider significance than
they would have had, if they had been, as largely

As tradition asserts, the work of David and Solomon alone; they reflect in singularly striking and attractive forms, springing out of the varied experiences of many men and many ages, different phases of the national religious life; in the Psalms we hear Israel's religious meditations, in the Proverbs the maxims of practical philosophy which its sages formulated, in Job and Ecclesiastes ponderings on the problems of life, in the Song of Songs an idyllic picture of faithful Hebrew love.

In what I have said I have indicated in outline—for details on an occasion such as the present are obviously impossible—the general character of the new light in which the Old Testament now appears; and I propose to devote the remainder of my time to considering three questions: (1) How do the facts I have referred to bear upon the inspiration of the Old Testament? (2) How do they affect the estimate which we form of its moral and doctrinal value? (3) What practical conclusions may be deduced from them? And the principle which, in answering these questions, I desire to emphasize is the existence of a *double element* in Scripture, a human not less than a Divine element, and the extreme importance, in view of the new knowledge which the present day has brought to bear upon the Bible, of recognizing *both* of these. An intelligible but mistaken reverence often prevents religious people from recognising properly the human element in the Bible;

and I wish to show how it is that the interests both of truth and of religion demand that the reality of this element should not be overlooked.

(1) With regard to the first of these questions, it is, I think, convenient to start with the formularies of the Church to which we individually belong. I naturally here speak primarily from the point of view of my own communion; but I believe that what I am about to say will be in accordance also with the formularies of those whom I am addressing. The formularies, both of the Church of England, and (unless I am greatly mistaken) of the Congregational Churches as well,* permit, in regard to inspiration, considerable freedom of individual opinion: they affirm the Scriptures to be of supreme authority in matters of faith; they specify certain doctrines, which they declare to be contained in the Scriptures, and to be the means of salvation; but they include no definition of inspiration: and while they define the books of which the Old Testament consists, they express no theory respecting either its literary structure, or the manner in which the Divine Will was communicated to its writers, or the stages by which, historically, revelation advanced.

The term inspiration is derived, of course, from the well-known passage in which St. Paul speaks of

* See the "Principles of Religion" of the Congregational Churches, in Curteis' *Bampton Lectures* (end of Lect. II).

Scripture as θεόπνευστος.* What, however, does this term denote ? or, to limit the question to the point which here concerns us, What are the necessary characteristics of a writing which is spoken of as "inspired" ? The use of the word will not guide us; for it occurs only in the passage referred to. Clearly the only course open to us is to examine, patiently and carefully, the book which is termed inspired, and ascertain what characters attach to it. Unhappily, a different course has often been followed. Men have assumed that they knew, as it were intuitively, what inspiration meant. They have framed theories without basis, either in Scripture itself or in the definitions of their Church, as to the notes, or conditions which must attend it; they have applied their theories forthwith to the Bible, and have demanded that it should conform to them. The theories of mechanical and verbal inspiration have indeed been now largely abandoned, as it is seen that they are too plainly inconsistent with the facts presented by the Bible itself. But other theories still prevalent are not less inconsistent with the facts. It is often supposed, for instance, that an inspired writing must be absolutely consistent in all its parts, and free from all discrepancy or error. But the Bible does not satisfy these requirements. I

* 2 Tim. iii. 16-17 : " Every scripture inspired of God is also profitable for teaching, for reproof, for correction, for instruction [or, discipline] which is in righteousness, that the man of God may be complete, furnished completely unto every good work."

may quote here the words of a speaker at the recent Church Congress: "I hope I shall not pain any one when I express my own opinion that the Bible is not free from imperfection, error, and mistake in matters of fact. Let me add that it is a conclusion to which I have slowly and reluctantly come."* The Bible, moreover, contains accommodations to an immature stage of religious practice or belief; even in the Psalms there are passages which cannot be appropriated by the followers of Christ. The Bible also exhibits other characteristics which we should not antecedently have expected to find in it. It contains double and divergent accounts of the same events. The history has in some cases been committed to writing a considerable time after its occurrence, and is thus probably presented to us in the form in which it has been gradually shaped by tradition. There are cogent reasons for believing that in some parts of the Old Testament we are not reading literal history, but history which has been idealized or, as in many parts of the Chronicles, transformed under the associations of a later age.† Elsewhere, again, literary considerations show that

* *Report of the Newcastle Church Congress* (1900), p. 154.

† The reference is to those narratives of Chronicles which are not,—like 1 Chr. x. 1-10, 2 Chr. x., for instance,—transcripts, almost unaltered, from the Books of Samuel, or Kings, but are the Chronicler's own composition, and reflect his own conception of the history. See the article on Chronicles in Hastings' *Dictionary of the Bible*; or the present writer's *Introduction to the Literature of the Old Testament*, pp. 493-502 (ed. 8, pp. 525-534).

E

sayings and discourses are strongly coloured by the individuality of the narrator; the writers themselves also afford indications that they are subject to the limitations of culture and knowledge imposed by the age in which they lived. *A priori*, no doubt, we might have expected these things to be otherwise; but our *à priori* conceptions of the works and ways of God are apt to be exceedingly at fault. The facts which I have referred to should not surprise us, or tempt us to doubt the authority of Scripture. They may help to refute a false theory of inspiration; they will be embraced and allowed for in a true theory. They belong to the human element in the Bible. They show, that as inspiration does not suppress the individuality of the Biblical writers, so it does not altogether neutralize human infirmities, or confer upon those who have been its instruments immunity from error. As the writer whom I have just quoted forcibly puts it, "Men argue that since the Bible is God's Word it must be free from all imperfection. The argument is equally valid that since it is man's word it cannot be thus free." Too often, it is to be feared, the explanations offered of the discrepancies and other difficulties of the Old Testament leave much to be desired, and are adapted to silence doubt rather than to satisfy it. But each time that this process is repeated the doubt reasserts itself with fresh strength. What wonder that there are men who, when they find that their beliefs about the Bible cannot be sustained without a succession of artificial and improbable suppositions, cast off the entire system with which, as they have been brought up to believe, these improbabilities are inseparably connected? It is a fatal mistake to approach the Bible with a preconceived theory of inspiration, or a theory formed irrespectively of the facts which it is called upon to explain. A theory of inspiration, if it is to be a sound one, ought to embrace and find room for all the characteristics displayed by the book which claims to be inspired.

The inerrancy of Scripture, as it is called,* is a principle which is nowhere asserted or claimed in Scripture itself. It is a principle which has been framed by theologians, presumably from a fear lest, if no such principle could be established, the authority of Scripture in matters of doctrine could not be sustained. The end is undoubtedly a sound one; but the principle by which it is sought to secure it is quite unable to support the weight which is laid upon it. In the past, probably, this was not apparent, but it is apparent now. We cannot honestly close our eyes to the facts contradicting it.† It is the *facts* which force upon us the necessity of a

* Though the expression is, perhaps, more familiar in America than in this country. See Dr. Briggs' *General Introduction to the Study of Holy Scripture* (1899), p. 615 ff.

† Comp. further on this subject Dr. F. Watson's volume, *Inspiration*, published by the S.P.C.K. in 1906, p, 234 ff.

revision of current theories of inspiration. It is true that, whether we are theologians or ordinary Christian men, it is the doctrines of Scripture that are of importance to us; it is the doctrines which are to form our guide in life, and our lode-star to eternity. But the truth of these doctrines will be best maintained if we judge Scripture by the canons of ordinary historical evidence. It certainly will not be maintained if we make it depend upon an artificial principle, which breaks down as soon as it is seriously put to the test. As I shall hope to show directly, the great theological verities taught in the Old Testament are absolutely untouched by critical investigation; while the documents on which the *specific* doctrines of Christianity rest are so different in their nature from those which are here concerned, that criticism, though it may in some cases modify the idea which we once held of their origin and structure, leaves the substance of them intact: in particular, the testimony to our blessed Lord's life and work is so much more nearly contemporary with the events recorded than can often be shown to be the case in the Old Testament, and also so much more varied and abundant, that, by an elementary principle of historical criticism, it is of proportionately higher value. It does not appear to me that the foundations of our faith are endangered either by the application of reasonable critical principles to the Old Testament, or by the adoption of a theory of inspiration which shall do justice to the facts that have to be accounted for.

(2) I pass now to the second question, viz., How do critical views of the Old Testament affect our estimate of its moral and doctrinal value? As I have just observed, the vital truths declared in the Bible appear to me to be wholly unaffected by critical inquiries, or critical conclusions, respecting its structure: criticism deals with the external form, or shell, in which these truths appear, the truths themselves lie beyond its range, and are not touched by it. It may be that individual critics reject some or even many of those truths which Christians, speaking generally, regard as vital; but that is not because they are critics, as such, but because they approach the subject with some anterior philosophical principles, and they would reject these truths whether they were, in the technical sense of the word, critics or not. The Christian critic starts with the belief that the Bible contains a revelation of God, and that its writers are inspired: his object is not to deny the revelation or the inspiration, but to ascertain, as far as possible, the conditions under which the revelation was made, the stages through which it passed, and the character and limits of the inspiration which guided the human agents through whom the revelation was made, or who recorded its successive stages. By inspiration I suppose we may understand a Divine afflatus which, with-

out superseding or suppressing the human faculties, but rather using them as its instruments, and so conferring upon Scripture its remarkable manifoldness and variety, enabled holy men of old to apprehend, and declare in different degrees, and in accordance with the needs and circumstances of particular ages or occasions, the mind and purpose of God. I say in different degrees, for it must be evident that the Old Testament does not in every part stand upon the same moral or spiritual plane, and is not everywhere in the same measure the expression of the Divine mind: inspiration did not always, in precisely the same degree, lift those who were its agents above the reach of human weakness and human ignorance. The Bible is like a lantern with many sides, some transparent, others more or less opaque, and the flame burning within does not shine through all with the same pure and clear brilliancy.* Or, to change the figure, there is room in the economy of revelation, as in the economy of nature, for that which is less perfect as well as for that which is more perfect, for vessels of less honour as well as for vessels of greater honour. Certainly, in a sense, every true and noble thought of man is inspired of God; the searchers after truth who in a remote past and in distant climes sought after God, in part also found Him; but with the

* The simile is that of an old Puritan divine, quoted by Dr. Briggs, *The Bible, the Church, and the Reason* (1892), p. 101.

# THE LIGHT OF TO-DAY

Biblical writers, the purifying and illuminating Spirit must have been present in some special and exceptional measure. Nevertheless, in the words of the prophet, or other inspired writer, there is a human element not less than a Divine element; it is a mistake, and a serious mistake, to ignore either. We may not, indeed, be able to analyse the physical conditions under which a consciousness of Divine truth was awakened in the prophets; but by whatever means the consciousness was aroused, the Divine element which it contained was assimilated by the prophet, and thus appears blended with the elements that were the expression of his own character and genius.

And so it is that the voice of God speaks to us from the Old Testament in manifold tones.* Through the history of Israel as a nation, through the lives of its representative men, and through the varied forms of its national literature, God has revealed Himself to the world. From the Old Testament we learn how God awakened in His ancient people the consciousness of Himself; and we hear one writer after another unfolding different aspects of His nature, and disclosing with increasing distinctness His gracious purposes towards man. In the pages of the prophets there shine forth, with ineffaceable lustre, those sublime declarations of righteousness, mercy, and judgment which have impressed all

* " By divers portions and in divers manners " (Heb. i. 1).

readers, to whatever age, or clime, or creed, they have belonged. In the Psalms we hear the devout human soul pouring forth its emotions in converse with God, declaring its penitence and contrition, its confidence and faith, its love and devotion, its thanksgiving and jubilation, its adoration and praise. In the Law, viewed in its different parts, we hear the voice of God accommodating itself to the needs of different ages, and disciplining His people by ordinances, sometimes imperfect in themselves, till they should be ready for the freedom to be conferred by Christ. The historians set before us, from different points of view, the successive stages in the Divine education of the race. They do not, like the prophets, claim to be delivering a message which they have received immediately from God: their inspiration is shown in the spirit which they breathe into the narrative and in their interpretation of the history; they show how a providential purpose overrules it; and they bring out the spiritual and moral lessons implicit in it. Sometimes, especially in dealing with the earlier period, to which no sure historical recollections reached back, they are dependent, doubtless, upon popular oral tradition; but penetrated as they are by deep moral and religious ideas, and possessing profound spiritual sensibilities, they so fill in the outlines furnished by tradition, that the events or personages of antiquity become spiritually significant—embody spiritual lessons, or become spiritual types, for the imitation or warning of succeeding generations. And like all other writers of the Old Testament, they declare very plainly God's approval of righteousness and His displeasure at sin. It is impossible not to believe that both the literature and the religious history of Israel would have been very different from what they were, had not some special *charisma* of supernatural insight into the ways of God been granted to its religious teachers.*

(3) Thirdly, I should like, if I may be allowed to do so, to offer some suggestions of a more or less practical character. A large amount of new light has been shed upon the Old Testament; our knowledge of the ways in which God of old time "spake to the fathers by the prophets" has been variously modified, corrected, or enlarged; and it is clearly our duty to turn this knowledge to some practical account. If, then, I may begin by addressing a few words more particularly to those of my hearers who may be regarded still as students and learners, I

* The subject of the preceding paragraphs has been developed by the writer more fully in the 6th and 7th of his *Sermons on Subjects connected with the Old Testament*, on " The Voice of God in the Old Testament," and " Inspiration," respectively. See also the comprehensive and illuminative treatment of the same subject in Prof. Sanday's *Bampton Lectures* on " Inspiration " (1893), esp. Lectures iii., iv., v. and viii. (A paragraph on the permanent religious value of the Old Testament, which originally followed here, has been omitted as no longer necessary, in view of the fuller treatment of the same subject in the next paper).

would observe that the foundation of all true Biblical study consists in a first-hand knowledge of the Bible itself, to be obtained, wherever possible, by a training in sound and scientific methods of philology and exegesis. Nothing can supersede an acquaintance, as intimate as it can be made, with the original languages of the Bible; it is that knowledge which brings us as nearly face to face as is possible with the original writers, and enables us to perceive many links of connexion and shades of meaning, which can with difficulty, if at all, be brought home to us by a translation. But we live in another world from that in which the Biblical writers moved; and hence the associations suggested by a given word, which were obvious at once to those who originally used it, or heard it used, are often not apparent to us; and they have to be recovered painfully and slowly, by research of various kinds, in geography, archæology, life and manners in the East, or other subjects, if the Bible is to speak, even approximately, with the same distinctness to us as it did to those to whom its various parts were originally addressed.

Philology and exegesis, assisted by such ancillary studies, form, then, the foundation of sound Biblical knowledge; but the next aspect under which, if it is to be intelligently understood, the Bible must be studied, is the *historical* aspect. The Bible is the embodiment of a historical revelation; and if the significance of the successive stages of this is to be adequately grasped, the different parts of the Bible must be viewed in their true historical perspective, in order that the correlation of the revelation to the history may be properly perceived, and the aims, and position, and influence of the different prophets, for instance, may be properly understood. This work can only be accomplished by criticism. And it is here that criticism, by distinguishing—as its name implies—what was once confused, has proved a most helpful handmaid of theology. There is a principle, the importance of which has long been recognized by theologians, the *progressiveness of revelation*, its adaptation, at different periods, to the moral and spiritual capacities of those to whom it was primarily addressed; and what is sometimes called the "higher criticism" (see above, p. 6) of the Old Testament, determining, as it does, at least approximately, the stages by which the Old Testament gradually reached its present form, enables the theologian to carry on and develop this principle to its legitimate consequences. A true historical view of the growth of the Old Testament, and of the progress of revelation, besides being important for its own sake, is valuable also in another way; it removes, viz., many of the difficulties, sometimes historical, sometimes moral, which the Old Testament presents, and which frequently form serious stumbling-blocks. The older apologists, by the harmonistic and other methods at their disposal, were quite unable to deal with these: historical criticism shows that they belong to the human element in the Bible, and that they are to be explained by reference either to the historical position of the writer, or to the imperfections incident to a relatively immature stage in the spiritual education of mankind.*

What conclusions reached by critics may, however, be reasonably accepted? I must here insist again upon a distinction, to the importance of which I have called attention elsewhere, because it appears to me to be one which is not always sufficiently kept in view. I mean the distinction between *degrees of probability*. The value and probability of a conclusion depends upon the nature of the grounds upon which it rests. Hence, I venture to think, it is a sound practical rule to acquire early the habit of *classifying* conclusions, of estimating them with reference to the grounds alleged on their behalf, and of asking ourselves, Is this practically certain? or, Is it only probable? or, Is it more than just possible? I should apply this rule pretty freely to emendations, to interpretations, to historical or archæological hypotheses, and to other similar subjects. Now, some of the conclusions reached by critics rest upon such a wide and varied induction of facts that they may be accepted as practically certain, and as de-

* Comp. Kirkpatrick, *The Divine Library of the Old Testament* (1891), pp. 103-109.

serving to be called the assured results of criticism. But beyond the limit of these assured results there is a tolerably wide fringe, in which, from the nature of the case, from the fact that the data are slight, or uncertain, or conflicting, no indisputable conclusions can be drawn; there is scope for more than one possibility; clever and even illuminative hypotheses may be suggested, but we cannot feel confident that they are correct. We must not resent hypotheses of this kind being propounded, even though in some cases they should seem to us improbable; for such hypotheses, in this as in other departments of knowledge, are one of the conditions on which progress depends. They mark out the lines upon which attention should be concentrated and investigation carried on, with the view, as the case may be, of either confirming or invalidating them. This fringe of uncertainty, as it may be called, forms an attractive field for speculation, and it frequently gives rise to rival hypotheses; but it is essential that it should be distinguished carefully from the field within which we may speak rightly of assured results being reached, and that conclusions relating to it should be adopted with caution and reserve. I may add that the differences between critics, which are sometimes laid indiscriminately to their charge, and spoken of as if they implied on their part the habitual use of false methods, are in reality limited to this margin of uncertainty, where their occurrence is simply a natural consequence of the imperfection or ambiguity of the data.

May I say, lastly, in what way, as it seems to me, the critical view of the Old Testament should be introduced into teaching ? As regards children, I do not think that on this ground any change whatever should be made in the manner in which they are taught; they are not in a position to understand the questions or distinctions involved. But they should be familiarized early with the text of the Bible: if I may speak from the experience of my own household, a text of the New Testament a day is learnt without effort by a child of six, and if the process is continued, a valuable selection of continuous passages from both Testaments may be known by heart by the age of nine or ten. Gradually, as the child grows older, it should be familiarized with the historical parts of the Bible, the narratives of the Gospels, the stories of the patriarchs, the Exodus, the Judges and Samuel. Whatever is to be added afterwards, a knowledge of the text is a primary essential, and of course simple lessons suggested by the narrative may be pointed out, for these lessons are there, whatever the historical character of the narrative should ultimately prove to be. But when the children reach an age at which their powers are maturing—and if they were boys in the upper classes of a public school, their mental outlook would be beginning to be enlarged, and they would be encour-

aged to inquire about many things which it would
not have occurred to them to inquire about before—
then I think that the principal conclusions reached
by scholars on the subject of the Old Testament
should be gradually and judiciously placed before
them. It does not seem to me to be right or just
that young men should be sent into the world with
antiquated and untenable ideas about the Bible,
which are no part of Christian doctrine, and are no
element in any creed, and so to run the risk of being
disillusioned, when the time comes, at unfriendly
hands, and of making shipwreck of their faith.* We
have our treasure in earthen vessels, and it is not
wise to imperil the treasure for the sake of the ves-
sel. The principal difficulties of the Bible do not, to
most minds, consist in the doctrines which it teaches,
but in the *historical setting* in which these doctrines
are often presented. This historical setting has, in
the cases I have in view, inherent improbabtlities,
entirely irrespective of the miraculous element in it,
and arising out of the representation itself; they
may consist, for instance, in false science, they may
consist in historical or literary inconsistencies: but
whatever they are, they are due to the human element in the Bible; and it is our duty to recognize

* On the disastrous effect of teaching the dogma—which, it is
to be observed, is entirely un-Biblical,—of the equal value and
validity of all parts of Scripture, without discrimination, comp.
the forcible remarks of G. A. Smith, and the testimony of Henry
Drummond, quoted by him, in his *Modern Criticism and Preaching
of the Old Testament* (1901), pp. 25-28.

this element, to discover its character and extent, and to show clearly that it does not enter into the creed of a Christian man in the same way in which the fundamental doctrines of the Bible do. In the Apostles' Creed, for instance, we confess our belief in God as the Maker of heaven and earth; but we do not affirm that He made it in the manner described in the first chapter of Genesis.

The Bible can never suffer by having the truth told about it. The Bible suffers, and religion suffers, when claims are made on its behalf which it never raises itself, and which, when examined impartially, are seen to be in patent contradiction with the facts. The undue exaltation of the human element in the Bible finds then its Nemesis. It ought, then, to be shown that the primary aim of the Bible is not to anticipate the discoveries of science, or to teach correct ancient history, but to teach moral and spiritual truths, and history only in so far as it is the vehicle or exponent of these. It ought, further, to be shown that the historical and literary character of the Old Testament writings is just a natural consequence of the conditions under which the authors wrote; those who lived nearer the events described being naturally, for instance, better informed than those who lived at a distance from them. No historical writer ever claims to derive the materials for his narrative from a supernatural source (cf. St. Luke i. 1-4); and so far as we are aware, it has not pleased God in

this respect to correct, where they existed, the imperfections attaching to the natural position of the
writer. Applying these principles, I should explain
how, in the opening chapters of Genesis, two writers
had told us how the Hebrews pictured to themselves
the beginnings of the world and the early history of
man; how, borrowing their materials in some cases
from popular tradition or belief, in others, directly or
indirectly, from the distant East, they had breathed
into them a new spirit, and constructed with their
aid narratives replete with noble and deep truths respecting God and man; how one writer had grafted
upon the false science of antiquity a dignified and
true picture of the relation of the world to God; how
another writer, in a striking symbolic narrative,
had described how man's moral capacity was awakened, put to the test, and failed; how in the sequel,
by other symbolic narratives, the progress of civilization, the growing power of sin, God's judgment upon
it, His purposes towards man, are successively set
forth.*  Passing next to the patriarchal period,
where real historical recollections seem to begin, I
should show how the skeleton, which is all that we
can reasonably suppose to have been furnished by
tradition, was clothed by the narrators with a living
vesture of circumstance, expression, and character,—

* Comp., for details, the small but instructive volume of Prof.
Ryle, of Cambridge (afterwards Bishop of Winchester, and now
(1911) Dean of Westminster), called *The Early Narratives of
Genesis* (1892).

F

being, no doubt, in the process coloured to some extent by the beliefs and associations of the age in which the narrators lived themselves,—and how in this way the pattern-figures of the patriarchs were created, and those idyllic narratives produced which have at once fascinated and instructed so many generations of men.* I should proceed similarly through the other parts of the Pentateuch, explaining, without concealment or disguise, the grounds which preclude us from accepting the narrative as uniformly historical, but pointing out that it was the form in which the Hebrews themselves told the story of the Exodus and of their conquest of Canaan, and emphasizing especially what is really its most important element, the religious teaching embodied in it,—for example the lessons suggested by the beautifully drawn character of Moses, and the many striking declarations which it contains of the character and purposes of God. I repeat it, the irreligious or unspiritual man may ignore all this; but no criticism can eliminate it from the narrative. I should also call attention to the three great codes of law contained in the Pentateuch,† indicating the general

---

* Comp. the articles on the different patriarchs in Hastings' *Dictionary of the Bible ;* or the present writer's *Book of Genesis,* pp. lxi.-lxxiv.

† The " Book of the Covenant" (Ex. xx. 23-xxiii.), Deuteronomy, and the Priestly Law (chiefly Leviticus and the greater part of Numbers). See. for further details, the article " Law in Old Testament," in Hastings' *Dictionary of the Bible.*

character and purpose of each, and dwelling in particular upon the lofty spiritual teaching of Deuteronomy. I should then, as occasion offered, select passages from the prophetical books, showing in what way they had a meaning and a significance in the circumstances, political or social, of the time at which they were written, and pointing out the permanent moral and spiritual lessons contained in them. I need hardly say that I should not meanwhile neglect the New Testament; but I am not dealing with that to-night. I do not understand that by teaching such as this the religious value or authority of the Old Testament would be depreciated or impaired: I believe, on the contrary, that its contents would gain very greatly in reality; it would be read with increased interest and appreciation, and the Divine element in it would be placed upon a far firmer and securer foundation than is provided for it by the ordinary view. The importance of improved methods in the Religious Teaching in Secondary Schools has been recently urged with much force, and, at the same time, with reason and discrimination, in a volume bearing this title by Dr. Bell, the Headmaster of Marlborough College. I am aware that, for the purposes I have indicated, the helps in the shape of commentaries and manuals which many teachers might require are at present fewer than they should be; but the claims of the Bible to be studied more intelligently, though at the same time not less reverently, than it used to be, have of late years been widely recognised in this country, and it is reasonable to expect that the deficiency in suitable books may in due time be supplied.*

* Since these words were originally written (in 1900) the expectation here expressed has been fulfilled to a gratifying extent. See the list of select books below, p. 89 ff.

# THE PERMANENT RELIGIOUS VALUE OF
# THE OLD TESTAMENT.

## IV.

## THE PERMANENT RELIGIOUS VALUE OF
## THE OLD TESTAMENT.*

IN an article such as the present, it is hardly necessary to say, it is impossible to treat a subject like
this with any approach to completeness. All that
I can do is to suggest briefly for the reader's consideration some of its more salient aspects, leaving
him to fill in details, and supply omissions, from the
knowledge of the Old Testament which he possesses
himself. I shall, therefore, without further preface,
proceed to summarize the chief heads under which,
as it seems to me, the elements of permanent religious value in the Old Testament may be grouped,
and so indicate the grounds which, even while its
contents are judged by a critical standard, must ever,
I believe, secure for it a position and influence in the
Church, second only to those possessed by the New
Testament itself.

I. The first and primary claim, then, to permanent
religious value which the Old Testament possesses
consists in the surprisingly lofty and elevated conceptions of God which prevail in it—conceptions,

* Reprinted from the *Interpreter* for January, 1905, p. 10 ff.

moreover, which appeal more strongly, and are more satisfying, to the religious instincts of mankind than those which are to be found in any other literature, save only in that of the New Testament. Of course, when this is said, it must be remembered that the revelation of God contained in the Old Testament advanced by stages and was gradual; and this being the case, it must at once be frankly admitted that in parts of the Old Testament there is an accommodation to the immature stage of religious belief which the people had reached, and that sometimes the narratives, and even occasionally the prophecies, are coloured by the specifically national, or, as they are sometimes called "particularistic" features, which were the result of the often hostile and antagonistic relations in which Israel stood to the heathen nations around it. But when every deduction has been made on these accounts, it remains that the general conception of God presented by the Old Testament is singularly dignified, lofty and spiritual. To take but one or two examples. The science of the first chapter of Genesis is the science of the age in which the chapter was written; but upon this imperfect, and in many respects false science, its author, under the influence of the Divine Spirit, has grafted a wonderfully sublime and spiritual representation of the Sovereign Author of nature, conceiving and presenting Him as a purely spiritual Being, who, moulding the material substance of the universe to His will, adapts the world gradually, by successive stages, to become the abode of lower and higher forms of life, and (ultimately) of beings endowed with reason, and who assigns to every living species upon it its proper office and function. The science of this chapter is antiquated: but the representation of the Divine action contained in it is not, and can never become, antiquated; it must ever remain as one of the priceless heirlooms which the people of Israel have bequeathed to the world. And so when we pass to the second and third chapters of the same book, though, it is true, we can hardly, any more than in the first chapter, be reading a literal history, we have brought before us, in a pictorial or symbolical form, adapted to the comprehension of the men for whose spiritual instruction the narrative was first written, deep thoughts about God and man—how man was created by God, and placed by Him in a position designed to develop his capabilities, and test his character; how he was at first innocent; how he became—as man must have become, whether in "Eden" or elsewhere, at some period of his existence—conscious of a moral law, but how temptation fell upon him, and he broke it. The fall of man, the great and terrible truth, the reality of which is evidenced both by history and by individual experience, is thus vividly and impressively brought home to each one of us. Man, however, the sequel teaches us, though punished by God, is not forsaken by Him, nor left, in his long conflict with evil, without hope of victory. The representation of God in these chapters is much more anthropomorphic than that in ch. i., and is evidently the expression of a more primitive stage of religious thought: a series of sensible acts is attributed to Him; He *plants*, *takes*, *sets*, etc., and the sound of His footsteps is heard as He walks in the garden; but even the reader of the present age does not feel that the fact at all materially detracts from the essentially spiritual character of the fundamental teaching which the narrative contains.

But we must leave the historical books and pass on to consider briefly what some of the prophets teach on the same subject. Amos, the earliest of the canonical prophets, proclaims that Jehovah, though He is in a special sense the God of Israel, is at the same time the God of all the families of the earth, under whose providence the Philistines migrated from Caphtor just as Israel migrated out of Egypt, who views all nations with an impartial eye, and visits Edom or Moab for its sin not less than Israel, and Israel, in spite of His choice of it, not less than Edom and Moab. Hosea is the prophet of religious emotion: his own nature is one of love; and Jehovah is to him pre-eminently the God of love, who has cherished His "son" with tenderness and affection, who is grieved by the coldness with which His love is requited, but who still loves His nation even while He finds Himself obliged to cast it from Him.

# VALUE OF THE OLD TESTAMENT

Isaiah dwells upon the holiness and majesty of Jehovah; and in imposing imagery, such as he alone
among the prophets can command, depicts Him as
manifesting Himself against all that is "proud and
lofty" in Judah, as controlling from His throne in
heaven the movements of the nations, or as striking
down in storm and tempest the serried hosts of
Assyria. And the great prophet of the Exile, the
author of the discourses which now form chapters
xl.-lxvi. of the book of Isaiah, preaches in language
more exalted and impressive than is to be found in
any other part of the Bible, the transcendence, the
omnipotence, the infinitude of Israel's God, the
First and the Last, the sole Creator and Sustainer of
the Universe, whose throne is indeed in the height
of heaven, but who stands, nevertheless, in intimate
relation with the earth, who is the high and lofty
one that inhabiteth eternity, but who dwells also
with the humble and contrite heart, and who has,
moreover, His purposes of grace, which, though they
are directed with special affection towards Israel,
comprehend within their ultimate scope all the kin-
dreds of the earth.

The idea of God presented in these and other
passages of the Old Testament is not arrived at by
a process of philosophic abstraction; it is the result,
we can only suppose, of a Divinely quickened intuition, which enabled the inspired thinkers and seers
of Israel gradually to elevate and purify their con-

ception of Him, and to discern, as history moved on, and their own spiritual perceptions were enlarged, new aspects of His being. To sum up, in very general terms, the teaching of the Old Testament on the nature and attributes of God, we may say that it represents Him as a personal Being, who, though depicted under the most anthropomorphic imagery, is nevertheless considered always as purely spiritual; who possesses a definite moral character, and is all-holy, all-just, and all-wise; who condescends to enter into relations of grace with His intelligent creatures; who loves man, and will in turn be loved by him; whose anger is aroused by sin, but who is gracious towards the repentant sinner; who manifests Himself in His redemptive purpose to Israel, and teaches His nation ever gradually to know Him better, and who deigns in the end to make known His salvation to the nations of the world at large.

II. Secondly, the Old Testament is of permanent value on account of the clearness and emphasis with which it proclaims the duty of man, both towards God and towards his fellow-men. Love and reverence, obedience and gratitude, penitence for sin and humility—these are, in brief, to be the determining principles of man's attitude towards God. Passages illustrating what has been said will occur to every reader of these pages. For our present purpose it will suffice to ask whether the whole duty of man can be more forcibly summed up than in the two well-known passages of Deuteronomy:—

"The LORD our God is one LORD: and thou shalt love the LORD thy God with all thine heart, and with all thy soul, and with all thy might" (vi. 4, 5).

And (x. 12, 13)—

"And now, Israel, what doth the LORD thy God require of thee, but to fear the LORD thy God, to walk in all his ways, and to love him, and to serve the LORD thy God with all thy heart, and with all thy soul, to keep the commandments of the LORD, and his statutes, which I command thee this day for thy good?"

Deuteronomy is a great book: as has been justly said, it is a book of national religion, and, accordingly, has some of the limitations of age and place stamped upon it; but it is at the same time a book of personal religion, and so of universal religion: and in these two passages one of the most fundamental principles of the writer is impressively propounded. Love to God, i.e., an all-absorbing sense of personal devotion to Him, is to be the primary spring of human action, the presiding genius of the Israelite's life. Jehovah, the author is ever eloquently insisting, is the only God, a pure and spiritual Being, who has loved Israel, and is worthy to receive Israel's undivided love in return. Israel is to be a nation holy to Him; its members are never to forget that they are the servants of a holy and lov-

77

ing God; and love is to be the guiding principle of
their conduct, whether towards God or man. And
thus Deuteronomy teaches the great truth that religion is concerned not only with the intellect and
the will, but that it involves equally the exercise and
right direction of the affections.

III. The duties of man to his fellow-men are not
in the Old Testament referred to any principle of
ethics, as such: they are justified by religious sanc-
tions; and the manner in which they are treated in
it may thus be fitly noticed here. The paramount
importance, not only of what may be termed the
more private or personal virtues, but also of the
great domestic and civil virtues, upon which the
happiness of the family and the welfare of the community depend, is throughout insisted on in the Old
Testament. Truthfulness, honesty, sincerity, justice,
humanity, philanthropy, disinterestedness, neigh-
bourly regard, sympathy with the unfortunate or
the oppressed, the refusal to injure another by word
or deed, cleanness of hands, purity of thought and
action, elevation of motive, singleness of purpose,—
these, and such as these, are the virtues which prophets, legislators, and psalmists are alike, in different
ways, ever inculcating or commending. And corres-
ponding to this high appreciation of moral qualities
there is its correlative,—a hatred of wrong-doing
and a profound sense of sin,—which is stamped, if
possible, yet more conspicuously upon the literature

of ancient Israel. A single quotation must suffice as an illustration: it shall be from the first of the prophets, Amos (viii. 4-7), whose righteous indignation is aroused by the avarice and injustice rampant about him :—

> "Hear this, O ye that would swallow up the needy,
>     And cause the poor of the land to fail,
> Saying, When will the new moon be gone, that
>         we may sell corn ?
>     And the sabbath, that we may set forth wheat ?
> Making the ephah small, and the shekel great,
>     And dealing falsely with balances of deceit;
> That we may buy the poor for silver,
>     And the needy for a pair of shoes,
>     And sell the refuse of the wheat.
> The LORD hath sworn by the majesty of Jacob,
>     Surely I will never forget any of their works."

Till the grinding down of the poor and commercial dishonesty are things of the past—a consummation, it is to be feared, still far distant—these words of the herdman of Tekoa will not be antiquated or out of date. More examples could readily be found (e.g., Is. i., v.). The prophets devote some of their finest and most impressive utterances to declaring, upon religious grounds, the claims of the moral law upon the obedience of mankind, and to the rebuke of vice and sin.

IV. The Old Testament is of permanent value in setting before us examples of characters, determined and moulded by the influence of their religion, which we may in different ways adopt as our models and strive to imitate. Of course, it is not pretended that the characters of the Old Testament are devoid of faults, or blameless. Some, for instance, are limited by the moral and spiritual conditions of the age in which they lived, others exhibit personal short-comings peculiar to themselves: but these faults are generally discoverable as such by the light of the principles laid down in the Old Testament itself, and none can certainly fail to be perceived by those who live under the higher light shed upon them by the Gospel. But it is impossible not to see how differ-ently most of the Old Testament characters would have felt and acted had they not been softened and refined by the mellowing influences of the religion of Jehovah. The leading Old Testament characters display in a word not virtues merely, but *graces*. In the historical books, for instance, such qualities as kindness and fidelity, modesty and simplicity, do-mestic affection and friendship, the discipline and repression of self, are abundantly exemplified: in the case of Moses, to take but a single example, what reader can fail to be impressed by the nobility and dignity, the disinterestedness and love for his people which he habitually displays? No doubt, in the case of those narratives which were committed to writing long after the personages lived whose doings they purport to describe, the details are not all strictly historical; and the picture not unfrequently reflects the narrator's ideal rather than the actual facts: but this circumstance does not detract from their *didactic* value: the characters thus drawn still possess a great typical significance; they are ideals of faith and virtue, highmindedness and goodness, as these and other similar virtues might display themselves in many different situations of life; they are spiritual types, delineated by the piety of an age which looked back upon, and idealized, the distant and heroic figures of the past. But they are not the less products of the religion of Israel, and they are not the less to be reckoned among the inestimable heirlooms by which the religion of Israel has enriched the world. The nucleus of fact contained in the Chronicler's picture of David's removal of the Ark to Zion, and his preparations for a Temple (1 Chron. xv., xvi., xxii.-xxix.), except in the few verses excerpted without material change from ` Sam. vi. 12-20, must be exceedingly small;* but nevertheless these chapters present an impressive *ideal* of a godly king, intent upon organizing worthily the public worship of his God, and expressing to Him the due homage of a devout and thankful heart. And in the biographies of the patriarchs, as told in the Book of Genesis—though here also it is difficult to escape the conclusion that the actual facts have been more or less idealized,—the lessons which they teach are none the less valuable. Truths and duties, especially those be-

* See the note above, p. 49.

longing to the "daily round and common task," such as we all need to learn, and continually through our lives have occasion to practise, are illustrated and enforced by anecdotes and narratives, which even the youngest can understand, and which can never cease to fascinate and enthral those who have once yielded themselves to their spell.*

V. The Old Testament is of unsurpassed value for devotional use and suggestiveness. And here our attention is attracted naturally, in the first instance, by the Book of Psalms, in which the ripest fruits of Israel's spiritual experience are gathered together, and the religious affections find their richest and completest expression. In the Psalms the soul is displayed in converse with God, disclosing to Him, in melodious accents, its manifold emotions, its hopes and fears, its desires and aspirations: we hear in them, for instance, the voices of despair and distress, of confession and supplication, of confidence and faith, of yearning for God's presence and spiritual communion with Him, of thanksgiving and exultation, of adoration and praise; we hear meditations on the great attributes of the Creator, on His hand as seen in nature and history, on the problems of human life, and on the pathos of human existence; and we hear all these notes uttered with a depth and an intensity, and withal with a chastened beauty of

* *The Book of Genesis*, by the present writer, p. lxxiv. See further, ibid., pp. lxi. ff., lxviii.-lxxiii.

diction and rhythm, which secure for the Psalter a unique position in religious literature. It is the characteristic of the Psalms that love, and reverence, and trust, and such-like sacred affections, are not, as in most other parts of the Old Testament, commanded or enjoined as a duty from without; they are set before us as exercised, as the practical response offered by the believing soul to the claims laid upon it by its Maker, as the spontaneous outcome of a heart stirred by devout emotions. There are sound and valid reasons for doubting whether the Psalms are as largely as is commonly supposed a product of the earlier period of Israel's history: but the spiritual power and originality of a particular Psalm is not dependent upon the date at which it was composed, or the author who wrote it; and there can be no doubt that, whatever may be the dates of individual Psalms, the Psalter, as a devotional manual, rightly enjoys the pre-eminence which has ever been attached to it, and that it can never lose the place which it has continuously held in the affections and devotions of the Church.

But though the devotional spirit finds its fullest and most familiar expression in the Psalter, it must not be supposed that it is confined to this part of the Old Testament. Many passages of Deuteronomy, of the prophets, and the Book of Job, for instance, are also naturally adapted to kindle religious emotion, and stir the devotional instincts. It will be sufficient here to refer to the motives of gratitude and devotion so often persuasively appealed to in the discourses of Deuteronomy, to the hymns in Isa. xxiv.—xxvii., so beautifully expressive of the joy, and hope, and trust, of the redeemed community of the future, to the eloquent and moving strain of thanksgiving, confession, and supplication, in which the prophet leads the devotions of his people in Is. lxiii. 7-lxiv. 12, and to many passages in the Book of Job, which express, with great poetical beauty, sometimes the sense of the Creator's omnipresence and vastness, sometimes deep truths respecting the scope and methods of God's providence, sometimes the pathetic longing of the patriarch for a removal of the barrier which seems to separate him from God. The freshness, the force, and the completeness with which the devotional side of religion finds expression in the Old Testament must, as long as man continues possessed of religious instincts, ensure for it a first place in the affections of all who know it, and effectually prevent it from ever losing its value in their eyes.

VI. The Old Testament possesses a peculiar value of its own on account of the great ideals of human life and society which it holds up before its readers. These ideals, delineated usually in brilliant colours, are a characteristic feature in the writings of the prophets, who love to picture to themselves the age in which, after the troubles of the present are ended, the Kingdom of God will be established upon earth; when human nature, freed from all sin and imperfection, and inspired by an innate devotion to God and right, is to be renovated and transformed; when human society, no longer harassed by the strife of opposing interests, or honey-combed by oppressions and abuses, is to be held together by the bonds of mutual friendship and regard; and when the nations of the world, laying aside their weapons of war, are to be united in a federation of peace under the suzerainty of the God of Israel (see, for instance, Hos. xiv.; Is. ii. 2-4, iv. 2-4, xi. 1-10, xix. 18-25, xxxii. 1-8, lx.; Jer. xxxi. 33-34; Zeph. iii. 11-17, etc.). It is only too true, alas! that these ideals remain still unfulfilled: the passions and wilfulness of human nature have proved in too many cases obstacles insuperable even by the influences of Christianity: but the world, since the advent of Christ, has at least made some advance; and meanwhile these ideals remain as inspiring visions, ever holding up before us the consummation which human endeavour should exert itself to realize, and which human society may one day hope to attain.

VII. We may notice, lastly, the great stress laid in the Old Testament upon a pure and spiritual religion. Mankind have in all ages shown a readiness to conform with the external offices of religion, while heedless of its spiritual precepts and of the claim which it makes to regulate their conduct and their life. The Jews, in whose law, taken as a whole, sacrifice and other ceremonial observances bulked largely, were prompt and even punctilious in the performance of such external rites: they thought that if they were sufficiently regular in their attendance at the Temple, and in keeping up the ceremonial observances of their religion, it was of little moment what their conduct in other respects might be; they were secure of Jehovah's favour (Jer. vii. 1-15). The prophets, on the other hand, insist emphatically that God requires the service of the heart; and that ritual observances, however scrupulously maintained, are of no value in His eyes, except as the expression of a right heart, and accompanied by integrity of life. It may suffice to quote one of the memorable utterances of the prophets on this subject. Amos (v. 21-24) speaking in Jehovah's name exclaims:

"I hate, I despise your feasts,
   And I take no delight in your solemn
      assemblies.
  Yea, though ye offer me your burnt-offerings and
    meal-offerings, I will not accept them;
   Neither will I regard the peace-offerings of
     your fat beasts.
  Take thou away from me the noise of thy songs;
   For I will not hear the melody of thy lyres.
  But let judgement roll down as waters,
   And righteousness as an ever-flowing stream."

A religion of the heart, a religion influencing morally the direction of men's thoughts and lives and

* See also Hos. vi. 6, Is. i. 10-17, Mic. vi. 6-8, Ps. l. 16-23.

actions, is also evidently the ideal which the Psalmists placed before themselves, as it is also the ideal
presented in the beautiful portrait of a godly and
noble-minded Israelite depicted in the thirty-first
chapter of the Book of Job. The time can never
come when the pure and elevated teaching of the
prophets and psalmists will not form a moral and
spiritual standard, recalling to men the real demands
which God makes of His worshippers, and exempli-
fying, in letters which all can read, the character
and conduct in which He truly delights.

And so there can surely be but one answer to the
question of the permanent religious value of the Old
Testament. The Old Testament Scriptures enshrine
truths of permanent and universal validity. They
depict, under majestic and vivid anthropomorphic
imagery, the spiritual character and attributes of
God. They contain a wonderful manifestation of His
grace and love, and of the working of His Spirit upon
the soul of man. They form a great and indispensable preparation for the coming of Christ. They
exhibit the earlier stages of a great redemptive process, the consummation of which is recorded in the
New Testament. They fix and exemplify all the car-
dinal qualities of the righteous and God-fearing man.
They insist upon the paramount claims of the moral
law on the obedience of mankind. They inculcate
with impressive eloquence the great domestic and
civic virtues on which the welfare of the community

87

depends; they denounce fearlessly vice and sin. The Old Testament Scriptures present examples of faith and conduct, of character and principle, in many varied circumstances of life, which we ourselves may adopt as our models, and strive to emulate. They propound, in opposition to all formalism, a standard of pure and spiritual religion. They lift us into an atmosphere of religious thought and feeling, which is the highest that man has ever reached, save in the pages of the New Testament. They hold up to us, in those pictures of a renovated human nature and transformed social state, which the prophets love to delineate, high and ennobling ideals of human life and society, upon which we linger with wonder and delight, as they open out before us the unbounded possibilities of the future. And all these great themes are set forth with a classic beauty and felicity of diction, and with a choice variety of literary form, which are no unimportant factors in the secret of their power over mankind.